OSTEOPOROSIS

OSTEOPOROSIS

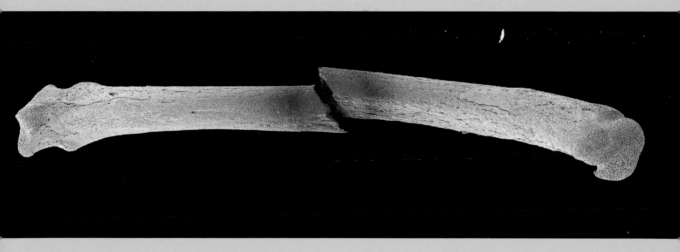

Gretchen Hoffmann

 **Marshall Cavendish**
Benchmark
New York

Special thanks to my two best editors, Bill and Karen, for all of their help and support.

With thanks to Renato N. Mascardo, M.D., FACE, FACP, Assistant Clinical Professor of Medicine, Division of Endocrinology & Metabolism, University of Connecticut School of Medicine, for his expert review of the manuscript.

Marshall Cavendish Benchmark
99 White Plains Road
Tarrytown, New York 10591-9001
www.marshallcavendish.us

This book is not intended for use as a substitute for advice, consultation, or treatment by a licensed medical practitioner. The reader is advised that no action of a medical nature should be taken without consultation with a licensed medical practitioner, including action that may seem to be indicated by the contents of this work, since individual circumstances vary and medical standards, knowledge, and practices change with time. The publisher, author, and medical consultants disclaim all liability and cannot be held responsible for any problems that may arise from use of this book.

Library of Congress Cataloging-in-Publication Data

Hoffmann, Gretchen.
    Osteoporosis / by Gretchen Hoffmann.
        p. cm. — (Health alert)
    Summary: "Discusses osteoporosis and its effects on people and
society"Provided by publisher.
    Includes bibliographical references and index.
    ISBN 978-0-7614-2702-5
    1. Osteoporosis—Juvenile literature. I. Title.
    RC931.O73H65 2008
    616.7'16—dc22

                        2007008787

Front cover: Computer artwork showing how osteoporosis can affect the spine
Title page: A fractured bone that has been weakened by osteoporosis

Photo research by Candlepants, Inc.
Front cover: Alfred Pasieka/Photo Researchers, Inc.
The photographs in this book are used by permission and through the courtesy of: Photo Researchers Inc.: Steve Gschmeissner, 3, 11; ESRF-CREATIS, 5 (detail), 41; SPL, 8; Gusto, 12; Hans-Ulrich Osterwalder, 15; CNRI, 16; David Scharf, 18; Jean-Paul Chassenet, 23; Professor Pietro M. Motta, 27; Larry Mulvehill, 28; Pasieka, 29; Sheila Terry, 36; Neil Borden, 40; Mauro Fermariello, 43; Russ Curtis, 44; Adam Gault, 47; AJPhoto, 49; Michelle Del Guercio, 52; Edward Kinsman, 54. PhotoTakeUSA.com: © Nucleus Medical Art, Inc, 13; © ISM, 17; © Yoav Levy, 45. Corbis: Joe McBride, 21; Michael Maslan Historic, 37; Rolf Bruderer, 51; Tom Stewart, 55. Art Resource, NY: Erich Lessing, 34. Super Stock: agefoto stock, 50.

Printed in China
6 5 4 3 2 1

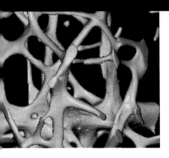

CONTENTS

1

WHAT IS IT LIKE TO HAVE OSTEOPOROSIS?

sabel was a seventy-year-old woman who was very healthy and active. She had five grandchildren whom she liked to chase around, and took long walks with her husband, Harold, nearly every afternoon.

One afternoon, as Isabel and Harold were on their way home from one of their strolls, Isabel stepped off the sidewalk to cross the street. She suddenly felt a sharp pain in her side, fell to the ground, and could not get back up. A neighbor called an ambulance, and Isabel was taken to the hospital. When they arrived at the hospital, the doctors explained that she had broken her right hip. (The hip bones are the bones on both side of the body, just below the waist. The hips are supposed to be strong and serve as the connecting point for the upper bone in each leg.)

When Isabel's family arrived at the hospital, they were shocked at what had happened. It was difficult to believe that something as simple as stepping off a curb could be enough to break such a sturdy bone. But the doctor explained that this can happen very easily when someone has osteoporosis, as Isabel did.

Osteoporosis is a disease that can weaken bones so much that even the slightest force can break them. For a person with osteoporosis, a powerful sneeze, a hug, or even just the action of walking down stairs can cause a bone to break. The word *osteoporosis* actually means "porous bone," or bone that is full of holes or pores. These holes make the bone too weak to withstand any pressure put on it. Osteoporosis can take away a person's mobility—the ability to move around easily. The disease can affect all the bones in the body, but is most common in the bones of the hip, **spine**, and wrist.

The doctors performed surgery on Isabel's hip. They repaired the bone so that she would be able to stand and walk again. Isabel was able to go home after spending several weeks in the hospital recovering from the operation. Isabel had a very hard time walking and often needed support—using a walker or help from another person—to move around. For months after the hip surgery, she had to go through **physical therapy,** where they helped her become stronger. Eventually, Isabel was able to walk without help.

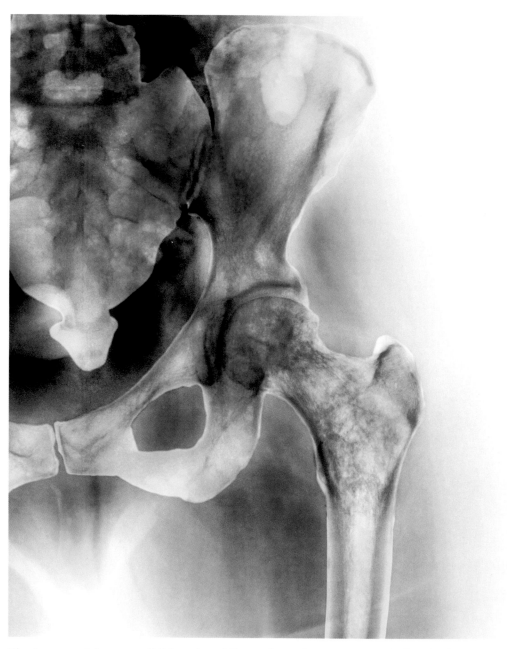

The brown patchy area of this colored X ray shows how osteoporosis has broken down parts of the thigh bone that connect to the hips. Bones that are weakened like this are more likely to break.

Once she found out she had osteoporosis, Isabel did everything she could to learn more about the disease. She found out what causes it, how it could have been prevented, and how to live comfortably with osteoporosis. She shared this information with her family so that her children and grandchildren would be careful about their health. As they learned more about osteoporosis, Isabel's younger family members changed their diets to more healthful ones and exercised regularly.

Isabel also changed some of her habits. She visited her doctors often so they could monitor her progress and check her other bones. Isabel had to make sure she was not doing anything that would be too hard on her bones. But she still enjoyed spending time with her grandchildren and continued to take walks with her husband. The osteoporosis changed her life, but Isabel would not let it control her life.

2

WHAT IS OSTEOPOROSIS?

If you have ever broken a bone, like one in your arm, leg, or hand, you know that it can be a very unpleasant experience. You might need surgery to fix the broken bone. And waiting for the break—called a **fracture**—to heal can be very frustrating. The pain can be anywhere from somewhat uncomfortable to very painful. Additionally, having broken bones makes many daily activities more difficult to do.

Once someone with osteoporosis breaks a bone, he or she is twice as likely to break another. In fact, every year in the United States more than 1.5 million bones are broken due to osteoporosis. Unfortunately, breaking a bone is often the first sign that someone has osteoporosis. It is sometimes called a silent disease because people can have osteoporosis without feeling sick or knowing something is wrong with their bones. Osteoporosis affects mostly older women, but it can also affect men and younger people.

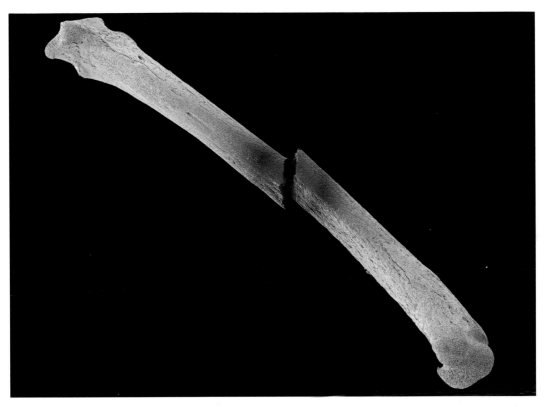

In this photograph of a fractured finger bone, the area colored in red shows where the bone was weakened by osteoporosis.

Osteoporosis was once thought of as an unavoidable result of getting older, but today doctors know that there are many things people can do to protect their bones. There are ways to detect the disease early and stop it from getting worse through diet, exercise, and medication. But the best idea is to prevent osteoporosis by building strong bones early in life and keeping them healthy as you grow older.

Strong bones support the body and allow you to stand, sit, play sports, and run. Without bones you could not move at all.

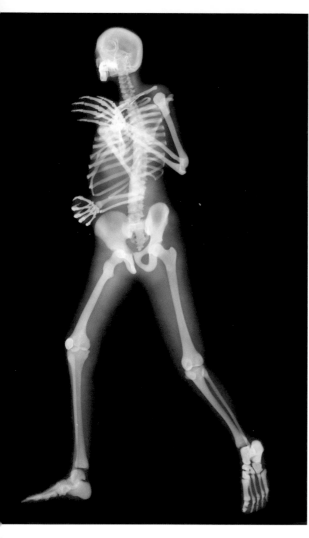

Your skeleton is the framework for the rest of your body. Without functioning bones, you would not be able to walk, run, or even stand.

Bones also protect the heart, lungs, brain, and other internal organs from injury. When you think of bones, you might picture a brittle skeleton like the ones used as Halloween decorations. In reality, bones are living tissues alive with active cells and flowing body fluids. Though they are hard, bones are constantly changing, and grow stronger with good nutrition and physical activity.

BONE STRUCTURE AND GROWTH

The bones of the skeleton are **dense** and strong, but they are not completely solid. The outside layer of bone is called **cortical bone.** This layer is mostly solid with only a few small open spaces. It resembles a brick wall, made with overlapping bone bricks set in layers. The insides of the bone are filled with **trabecular bone,** which looks like a sponge or honeycomb with many open spaces. The spaces within the trabecular bone are filled with **bone marrow** cells.

Bones are made mostly of a **protein** called **collagen.** Collagen provides the bones with a flexible framework. The strength and stiffness of bones comes from **calcium** compounds that make the collagen framework harder. This combination makes bones both flexible and strong enough to handle the stress that our bodies put on them.

Building strong bones—while you are growing—involves adding new bone material so that bones can grow and change in size

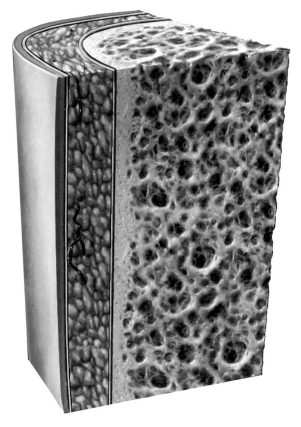

This illustration shows the different layers of bone. The trabecular bone is shown at the far right. Next to that is the hard layer of cortical bone. Fat cells and muscle tissue cover the outer layer of bone. The fat and muscle is then covered by skin.

and shape. This is similar to building a house—the house's initial framework and walls go up where there was once empty space. The rest of the house is built, with the framework and walls supporting the structures. This is similar to your skeleton. The bones of your skeleton serve as the framework for other parts of your body—inside and out.

Another natural process that occurs in the bones is called **remodeling.** In this process, old bone is taken away and new bone material is added to take its place. Bone remodeling is much like remodeling a room in a house. The structure is already in place, but you can update and replace old things with newer material. Bones are constantly renewed through this remodeling process.

Old or damaged bone is removed by a special kind of cell called an **osteoclast.** These large cells look like they have ruffled edges when viewed under a microscope. Their job of taking away bone is called resorption. Osteoclasts dig out a patch of old bone by actually dissolving the hardened minerals and collagen that make up the bone structure. The cavity—or hole—left by the osteoclasts is like a pothole in the pavement of a street. The hole in the bone gets filled in with new bone material by different cells called **osteoblasts.** Osteoblasts are responsible for the formation of new bone, like construction workers whose job it is to fill the potholes in the street. These rectangular-shaped cells make a lot of protein (like collagen) that is needed to make new bone material called **osteoid.** Osteoid is newly formed bone that only contains the protein collagen and does not yet have calcium added to harden it.

A computer illustration shows one of the processes involved in bone remodeling. The osteoclast (shown in green) is destroying bone that is damaged or needs to be replaced. After the osteoclast is done, osteoblasts will rebuild the bone tissue.

The osteoblasts work as teams to fill the cavity with new osteoid. Their next job is to direct the addition of calcium and other minerals that will harden the new bone. After these two jobs are done, osteoblasts flatten out and line the surface of the bone.

The digging done by osteoclasts happens much faster than repair work done by osteoblasts. It takes about three weeks to make a cavity, and about three months to fill it back in. Both types of cells continue to work during your entire

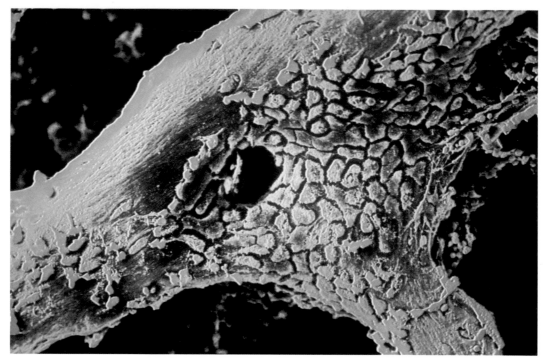

As part of the remodeling process, osteoblasts produce new bone material called osteoid. After the osteoid is produced, it hardens to form strong bone tissue.

lifetime. In fact, your whole skeleton will have been broken down and rebuilt by the work of osteoclasts and osteoblasts every ten years.

Scientists are studying how your body knows when and where bone damage has occurred. Somehow your body also senses how much bone needs to be replaced. Researchers think that bone cells called **osteocytes** are involved in this. Osteocytes are actually osteoblasts that became stuck in the newly created bone. Instead of building bone, their new job is to sense signals that tell them a part of the bone needs to be remodeled. Scientists think that trapped osteocytes form a connected communication network that think can detect when a part of the bone becomes deformed or damaged. Osteocytes then send a message to osteoclasts and osteoblasts through the cells lining the bone surface. The message tells the bone cells to start the remodeling process.

When a person is actively growing, during childhood and teenage years, more bone material is added and less is taken away. During this time the child's bones become larger, heavier, and denser. When a person is between twenty or thirty years old, his or her bones are as strong as they will

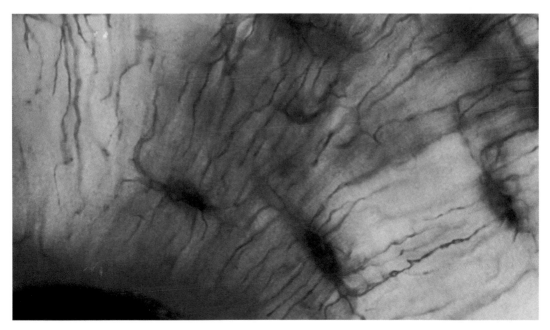

The osteocytes in this magnified photograph are shown in dark red.

Types of Bone Cells

Osteo is the Greek word for bone, and that is why all these cell types begin with "osteo."

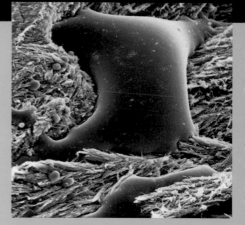

Osteoclasts (purple) are surrounded by collagen from bone tissue that the osteoclasts are breaking down.

OSTEOCLASTS

What they do:	Dissolve bone
Where they come from:	The bone marrow
Location in bone:	On the surface of the bone next to the dissolving bone

OSTEOBLASTS

What they do:	Work in teams to build new bone called osteoid, which is made of bone collagen and other proteins. Also direct the cells where to deposit calcium and minerals.
Where they come from:	Bone marrow
Location in bone:	On the surface of new bone

LINING CELLS

What they do:	Line the surface of the bone, and control the passage of calcium into and out of the bone. Make special proteins that activate the osteoclasts.
Where they come from:	Osteoblasts that have finished their job and have been flattened
Location in bone:	Lining the surface of bone

OSTEOCYTES

What they do:	Sense damage in the bone and help to direct where osteoclasts will dissolve old or damaged bone.
Where they come from:	Osteoblasts that turn into osteocytes while new bone is being formed. Osteocytes are surrounded by new bone.
Location in bone:	Inside the bone, connected to other osteocytes by long branches

ever be. This is known as **peak bone mass,** which means the maximum strength and density a person's bones will have during his or her entire lifetime. By the time the person is finished growing—during the late teens—around 90 percent of peak bone mass will be established. Bone mass and bone density are different terms that mean the same thing. They describe how strong bones are based on how much bone material is packed into a certain space.

The level of peak bone mass that is possible in any individual depends on several things. For example, men generally have higher peak bone mass than women. Also, people who have always been physically active have more bone mass than those who are not very active. Peak bone mass is important because people with higher peak bone mass have lower risks for osteoporosis later in life.

Once peak bone mass is achieved, the rates of dissolving old bone and building new bone are approximately equal for many years. During that time, bones do not change much in size, shape, or density. But slowly, over time, the body begins to remove more bone than it replaces.

BUILDING STRONG BONES

There are three major things your body needs for strong, healthy bones: physical activity, calcium, and **vitamin D.**

Physical activity

When you exercise or lift weights, your muscles become firmer and stronger. The same thing happens to your bones, except you cannot see the effects of exercise on bones the same way you can see strong muscles getting bigger. When an athlete curls his arm to show off his muscle, you can easily see how strong and firm the muscle is. But if you could see inside the arm you would see that the athlete's bones are big and strong too. Through physical activity, the athlete's body has strengthened the bones.

This is especially true for activities called **weight-bearing exercise.** These are exercises that make your body work against the force of gravity—your body is bearing or handling weight. Lifting weights uses muscular strength, but it also builds bone density and strength. After all, if your muscles did not have the framework of your bones, they would not be able to handle any weight at all. Jogging, walking, dancing, playing soccer or tennis, and jumping are all types of weight-bearing exercise.

For example, when you swing a tennis racquet, run across the court, jump to reach a ball flying over your head, or serve the ball, your body sends chemical messages to the bones in your arms and legs. These messages tell the bones to get ready to handle the repeated weight and impact of

Besides helping your overall health, playing sports, such as tennis, helps to make your growing bones stronger.

those actions. The more demands you place on your bones, the stronger they become. In fact, right-handed people who use their right arm for most sports and activities have slightly larger, stronger bones in their right arm compared to their left arm.

It is recommended that children get at least an hour of physical activity each day to build healthy, strong bones. Adults should also do strength-building and weight-bearing activities to keep bones strong.

Some exercises are good for your overall health, but are not weight bearing, and do not build bone density. During these activities the body is supported by something else and your bones do not feel as much stress. For example, in bicycling and swimming, your body is supported by a bike or by water. A doctor or health professional can advise you on what types of exercise are ideal for your age and physical activity level.

Calcium

Calcium is the most plentiful mineral found in the human body. On average, 2 percent of an adult's total body weight is from calcium stored in the body. Your bones are like a bank account for calcium. You make deposits to that account with the calcium in the food you eat. About 99 percent of that calcium is found in bones and teeth. The remaining 1 percent is found in the blood, **nerve cells,** and body tissues. Although your bones and teeth use up most of the calcium, it is also needed by the heart, muscles, and nerves to be able to work properly. You also need calcium to help your blood clot—or thicken—after an injury like a scrape or cut. Clotting helps to form a scab so you stop bleeding and your body can heal.

If you do not have enough calcium available for these other functions, your body will withdraw it from your bones. This is like withdrawing money from your bank account, except the money was being saved to buy something else that you needed. In the same way, the calcium in your bones is supposed to be used for your bone strength and development. Removing calcium from bones for use in the rest of the body weakens existing bone. It also prevents the formation of new strong bone. It is important to get the recommended amount of calcium each day so that you always have enough in your "account."

Young people between the ages of nine and eighteen need the most calcium of any age group. They need about 1,300 milligrams (mg) of calcium per day. Studies have shown that most people do not get enough calcium, especially during the years that they need it most. A national nutrition survey showed that only 19 percent of teenage girls and 52 percent

Dairy products, such as milk, cheese, and yogurt, are good sources of calcium.

of teenage boys are getting the recommended amount of calcium each day. The survey estimated that teenage girls in the United States take in an average of 740 mg of calcium each day—only about half as much as they should get.

There are many ways to get enough calcium into your diet, including dairy products and dark green vegetables that are naturally rich in calcium. Other foods, such as cereals, juices, breads, and tofu, can be fortified with calcium. This means that extra calcium has been added to the food when it was made or packaged. Most people take daily vitamin supplements. These supplements often have calcium.

Many doctors say that dairy products, such as milk and cheese, are the best way to get calcium. But many people avoid dairy products because they are watching their weight and think that whole milk or heavy cheese will be too much for them. Choosing low-fat milk and dairy products are excellent ways to get the needed calcium. In fact, skim milk and whole milk have about the same amount of calcium (300 mg), even though whole milk has more fat and calories per glass. Some people cannot eat dairy products because those foods make them sick. If this is the case, then they can most likely get their required calcium from other calcium-rich foods. A doctor or nutritionist can offer good advice on a healthy and balanced diet.

Calcium in Food

....

Food and Serving Size	Approximate Amount of Calcium per Serving
Milk (8 oz)	300 mg
Cheddar cheese (1 oz)	200 mg
Broccoli, uncooked (1 cup)	90 mg
Sardines (3.75 oz)	350 mg
Frozen yogurt ($\frac{1}{2}$ cup)	100 mg
Soybeans (1 cup)	260 mg
Cottage cheese (1 cup)	130 mg
Low-fat yogurt (8 oz)	330 to 450 mg
Almonds (1 oz)	75 mg
Fortified orange juice (8 oz)	300 mg
Tofu ($\frac{1}{2}$ cup)	200 mg
Turnip or collard greens (1 cup)	200–225 mg
Dried figs (10 figs)	270 mg
Baked beans (1 cup)	140 mg

Here are some easy and healthy ways to incorporate more calcium into your diet:
• Make oatmeal with low-fat milk instead of water for breakfast or a snack
• Snack on low-fat cheese snacks or string cheese
• Blend low-fat milk or yogurt with fruit and ice for a delicious smoothie
• Whip up some pudding with low-fat milk for dessert
• Top salads, soups, or sandwiches with low-fat cheese
• Pack a small bag of almonds for a snack on the go
• Have stir-fried tofu, broccoli, and other vegetables for a delicious dinner

Vitamin D

Vitamin D helps your body absorb calcium you get from food. This usually happens in your intestines—a part of the digestive system. Without vitamin D, your body is not able to get enough calcium and is forced to borrow calcium from the bones.

You should get the necessary amounts of vitamin D from a healthy diet. Vitamin D comes from food, such as egg yolks, saltwater fish, and liver. Some food products are fortified with vitamin D, which means the vitamin has been added.

Spending time outdoors in the Sun can also help your bones. When your skin is exposed to the Sun, your body produces another type of vitamin D. Unlike the vitamin D found in food, this type of vitamin D is a **hormone,** which is a chemical substance that travels through the blood to cause biological actions. These actions include strengthening the bones. But you should be very careful about how much time you spend in the Sun. Avoid overexposure and always protect your skin with the right amount of sunblock.

WHAT IS OSTEOPOROSIS?

As its name suggests, osteoporosis occurs when the bones have been weakened. The rate of bone deterioration is higher than replacement. What this means is that the bone cells

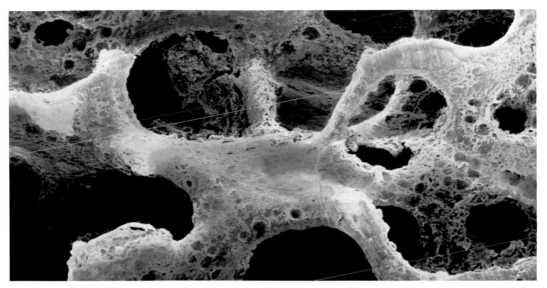

A magnified photograph shows bone tissue that has been weakened by osteoporosis. If the osteoblasts cannot replace and repair the weakened bone, the existing holes will get bigger, and more holes will form.

are not able to repair and strengthen the bones fast enough. As a result, large holes form in the bones. These holes can be found in both cortical and trabecular bone. Eventually, there are too many channels and cavities that have not been patched with strong new bone. The bones of the skeleton can no longer support the weight and strain the body puts on them. That is when the bone breaks. A fracture can happen with very little force because the bones are so badly damaged.

Besides bone fractures, osteoporosis can cause other health problems. Osteoporosis can cause severe back pain. It can also change a person's posture, which is the way you hold your body upright when standing or sitting. The bones in the spine are called the vertebrae. Osteoporosis in the vertebrae can make them so weak that they break and crunch down on one another. This changes the way the backbone curves and can end up looking like a hump sticking out of the person's upper back. Doctors refer to this curvature of the spine as **kyphosis.** In severe cases, a person with this problem may appear bent over all the time, like he or she is always looking at the ground. For some, this condition can be very painful.

Some people with osteoporosis actually shrink. They become several inches shorter than they used to be because

The abnormal curving of the spine caused by osteoporosis makes it impossible for some people to stand up completely straight.

the vertebrae have collapsed onto each other, and changed the shape and length of the spine. As a result, the person does not stand as tall as they once did. It can also make it harder to eat and breathe because the space inside the body for organs, such as the lungs and stomach, becomes smaller.

WHO IS AT RISK?

Osteoporosis affects certain types of people more often than others. There are some things that put a person at risk for osteoporosis that cannot be changed. One is being a woman. Two out of every three people who develop osteoporosis are women. Women are more likely than men to develop osteoporosis

The bones of the hip, spine, and wrist are the most common places that osteoporosis develops and fractures occur, but it can happen in any bone. Osteoporosis can also affect bones in the legs, arms, or the ribs. More than 90 percent of hip fractures are associated with osteoporosis. Approximately 700,000 vertebral (back) fractures and 300,000 hip fractures happen in people with osteoporosis in the United States each year.

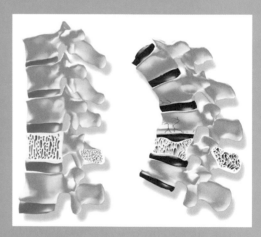

The illustration on the left shows five vertebrae of a healthy spine. The illustration on the right shows those same five vertebrae after osteoporosis sets in. The spine starts to curve, which makes a person hunch over.

Osteoporosis Statistics

....

More than 10 million people in the United States already have osteoporosis. Another 34 million are at high risk of developing the disease because their bones are becoming dangerously weak. Of the people with osteoporosis, approximately 8 million are women and 2 million are men. Researchers estimate that approximately $18 billion is spent each year in the United States on the treatment of osteoporosis and related injuries. The costs of osteoporosis will keep rising as more and more people develop the disease. The National Osteoporosis Foundation predicts that more than 61 million men and women older than age 50 will either have osteoporosis or be at high risk by the year 2020.

later in life because they go through a biological change called **menopause.** This occurs when women—usually older than fifty—no longer have menstrual cycles and can no longer give birth to children. The hormones produced inside their bodies change dramatically. One of the most important hormones in women is estrogen. Estrogen affects cells and systems throughout the body, and one of its roles is to tell the body to make bones strong and dense. During and after menopause, levels of estrogen drop and women tend to lose a lot of the bone strength they had built up throughout their lives. Men do not go through menopause, and so they never experience a time in their lives when such a dramatic change occurs in their bones. Bone loss for men is a more gradual process. That is why fewer men than women eventually develop osteoporosis. However, many older men in their seventies do experience changes in their hormones, which can lead to osteoporosis.

Another risk factor that people cannot control is older age. Osteoporosis is an age-related disease and usually affects adults older than age fifty. By age sixty-five or seventy, men and women lose bone mass at the same rate. But osteoporosis does not affect all older people. And younger people can also develop osteoporosis. Having other family members with a history of osteoporosis puts a person at increased risk for developing the disease. Being very thin or having a naturally small frame is also associated with an increased risk of developing osteoporosis. People with small frames are more likely to develop osteoporosis because they have smaller bones and less bone mass to begin with. Their bones will weaken more rapidly as material is taken away from bones that are already less dense. Some ethnic groups are at higher risk for developing osteoporosis. Caucasians and Asians are at higher risk, but other groups such as African Americans and Latinos are still at risk too.

Gender, older age, family history, having a small frame, and ethnicity are all risk factors that cannot be changed. But there are controllable risk factors that increase a person's chance of developing osteoporosis. One example is smoking.

Smoking is associated with a higher risk of developing osteoporosis. This is because the chemicals found in tobacco, like nicotine, are toxic or poisonous to bones. These chemicals may reduce the ability to absorb calcium and other nutrients from food. Researchers think that smoking may also slow down the growth of bone-producing osteoblasts.

Drinking a lot of alcohol can also increase the risk of osteoporosis. Alcohol can stop the absorption of calcium in the intestines. It can also stop the process that makes vitamin D active in the body. People under the influence of alcohol are also more likely to lose their balance, fall, and fracture a bone.

Being physically inactive also contributes to weak bones because bones need physical activity to develop strength. Some people choose not to be active. They would rather not exercise or do any physical activities. Sometimes people do not have a choice, and must stay off their feet because of surgery or illness. Either way, inactive people run a higher chance of developing osteoporosis because bones that are not used to walk, run, lift, or play will lose strength.

Often, people with osteoporosis become worried about breaking a bone, or breaking another bone if they have already had a fracture. They may cut down on their physical activity to avoid injury, but this is not always a good thing. People with osteoporosis should still get exercise to promote healthy bones. They can and should continue to do safe activities that they discuss with their doctor.

Not getting enough calcium or vitamin D through the foods you eat or drink also leads to unhealthy bones. People with eating disorders, such as anorexia, are at higher risk for osteoporosis. People with anorexia do not get enough calcium and other nutrients from the very small amount of food they eat.

There are also some types of medication that can increase the risk of osteoporosis. People may need to take these drugs for other conditions, and they should work with their doctor to make sure they also protect their bone health as much as possible. For example, people with arthritis, a painful condition that affects the joints where bones come together, may need to take certain medications. But these drugs can interfere with the way your body processes minerals like calcium and decrease bone formation.

Although osteoporosis can be treated with medication, preventing this disease is the best way to protect your bones. Building strong bones during youth is essential for preventing osteoporosis. Having healthy eating habits will provide your body with plenty of calcium, and vitamin D will help build strong bones. Being physically active will challenge your bones to be as strong as possible so that they will stay that way throughout your lifetime.

3

THE HISTORY OF OSTEOPOROSIS

Even before people fully understood what our bones, organs, and body fluids were made of and how they worked together, human beings were curious about their bodies. The study of anatomy—the science of understanding the body's organs and structures—began at least as early as 1600 BCE in Egypt. Later, Greek scientists played an important role gaining and sharing knowledge about the anatomy of animals and humans.

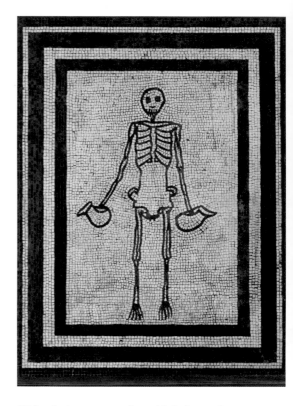

This skeleton mosaic, which is made up of tiles, was created by artists who lived in Italy around 100 to 300 CE. Doctors and scientists who lived more than a thousand years ago knew that the bones inside the body make up a complex framework.

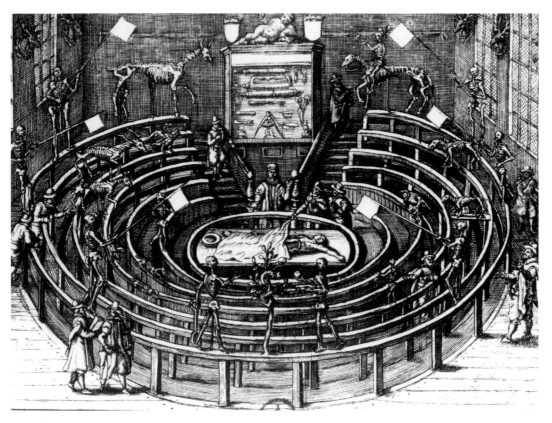

People studied the bodies of animals and humans by cutting them open after death, which is called dissection. Students and researchers still use dissection as a tool to understand how the body's systems work, but today we have much better tools and methods than early scientists did.

Early scientists and physicians discussed the form and function of the skeleton and gained knowledge by separating it from the rest of the body. There were many things that they did not understand about the way bones were formed or how to keep bones healthy. But as time progressed, they learned more and more.

DISCOVERING THE DISEASE

There is evidence that osteoporosis has affected people for thousands of years. Scientists have found mummies in Egypt with curved spines, most likely due to this disease. Paintings from the fifteenth century show elderly women stooped over or with hunched backs, probably due to curvature of the spine from osteoporosis. This change in posture that can happen to someone with osteoporosis is referred to as a "dowager's hump" in different works of

John Hunter made many new discoveries that helped improve surgery and other medical procedures used to treat illness.

literature. (A dowager is an older term for an elderly woman.)

Although the evidence of osteoporosis can be seen in these examples, people did not know very much about what caused the condition, or how to prevent or treat it, until recently. In England during the 1770s, a surgeon named John Hunter studied how bones grow and develop. He did experiments using animals and also studied changes in the human jaw bone. He was the first to describe the process of remodeling—that old bone is destroyed and new bone is created. Dr. Hunter lived in the time before microscopes were widely used, so he could not look closer to see the bone cells that are responsible for this process. Doctors did not consider osteoporosis a disease during Hunter's lifetime, and would not for more than 100 years after his death.

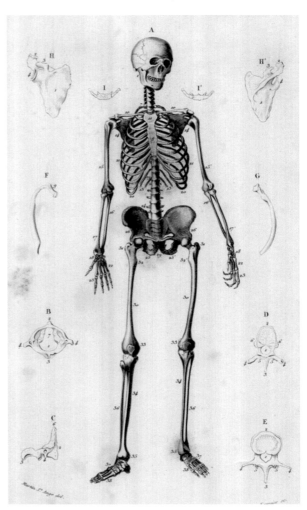

Jean Georges Lobstein, a French physician, is credited for naming osteoporosis in the 1830s. He noticed that some of his patient's bones had larger-than-normal holes. He used the term osteoporosis to describe what he saw, but did not further describe what might be causing these holes. Lobstein did not consider it to be a symptom of a disease.

This detailed illustration of the human skeleton was published in a French reference book from the 1840s.

MORE DISCOVERIES

Finally, in the 1930s and 1940s, Fuller Albright from the Massachusetts General Hospital realized that women who had gone through menopause were more likely to develop frail bones. To test his theory that loss of estrogen is associated with bone loss, he injected estrogen into pigeons and observed that their bone mass increased significantly. Dr. Albright proposed that the loss of estrogen at menopause causes a loss of bone because more bone is broken down than is created. He defined this disease as postmenopausal osteoporosis (meaning osteoporosis after menopause), and began treating all of his patients with estrogen.

Just as Dr. Hunter lacked the technology of microscopes to see the cells responsible for bone remodeling, Dr. Albright could not detect which of his patients had severe bone loss unless they already had symptoms such as broken bones or a curved spine. His solution was to treat them all.

Starting in the 1960s, researchers developed the tools to measure bone mineral density. Screening for osteoporosis became easier and more common. Improved technology and a better understanding of the disease also yielded better treatments. Scientists learned that men could also be affected by the disease. And rather than injecting estrogen into everyone with osteoporosis, new medications were developed

The Invention of the X Ray

Before the invention of the X ray, medical diagnosis was based on what the physician could see, touch, and hear to investigate the problem. Even the most experienced and skilled doctors could make mistakes or miss a patient's real problem. They needed a way to see inside the body without cutting into it.

In 1895, the German scientist Wilhelm Conrad Roentgen made a discovery that allowed doctors to take a look inside their patients without doing surgery. He discovered a new kind of ray that could pass through most materials, such as books and playing cards, but not others, such as metal weights or a lead pipe. While experimenting with this new discovery, Dr. Roentgen also found that he was able to use these rays to produce an image of the bones in his hand. That meant the rays could pass through skin and muscle, but could not go through the bones.

He referred to these mystery rays as "X" rays because he could not identify the source. However, the name stuck and we still refer to them as X rays today. Years later, scientists realized that the radiation—energy released in the form of particles or electromagnetic waves—produced during the X-ray process could be dangerous. When used too much or not properly, X rays could cause illnesses. Researchers worked to improve X-ray machines and techniques, and were able to make the process safer for both the patient and person running the machine. As technology improved, the images produced by the machines became clearer.

The discovery of X rays improved the way doctors were able to diagnose and treat diseases and other medical conditions. X rays are also used in more than just medicine. For example, X-ray machines are used for security in airports to check the contents of luggage being brought onto planes by passengers.

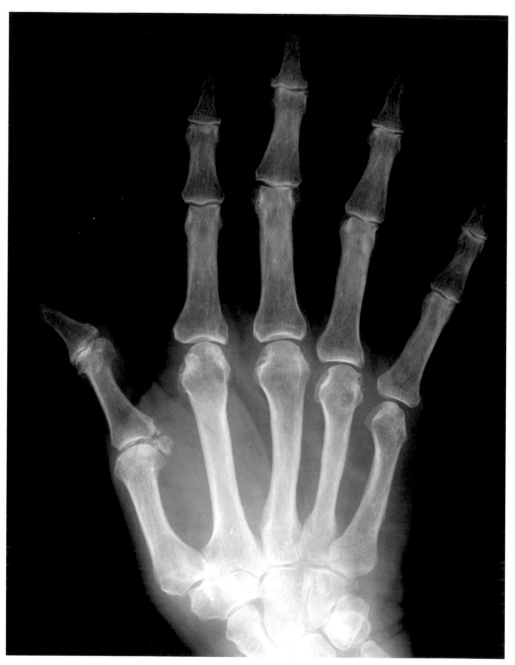

X rays allow doctors to closely examine human bones.

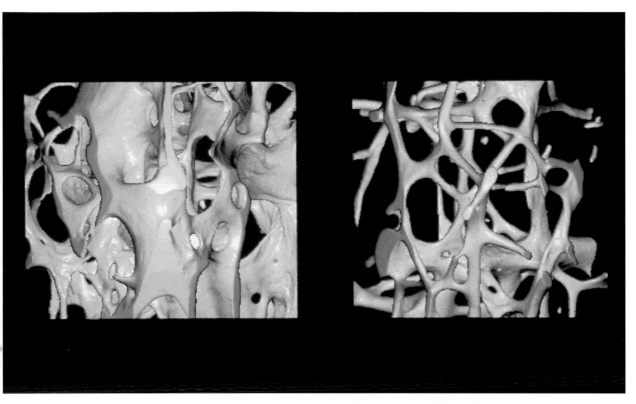

New technologies help doctors learn more about treating bone conditions like osteoporosis. This computer image was developed using special X rays of the vertebrae of a fifty-year old (left) and a seventy-year old (right). The bones of the seventy-year old have deteriorated because of osteoporosis.

to help replace lost bone cells. Prevention also became a more important part of dealing with osteoporosis. Doctors can now instruct patients on ways to help slow down or prevent the effects of osteoporosis.

4

DIAGNOSING AND TREATING OSTEOPOROSIS

Until recently, doctors did not know very much about how to prevent or treat bone disease. Many doctors believed that weak or broken bones were an unavoidable part of old age. Today we know much more about how to recognize, prevent, and treat osteoporosis.

DIAGNOSIS

Considering the first sign of osteoporosis is often a broken bone, people at risk for osteoporosis should have their bone health tested before a fracture occurs. Osteoporosis can be easily detected and diagnosed early in the disease by a safe and painless bone mineral density test. Physicians recommend that all women should have a bone mineral density test by the time they are sixty-five years old, or younger if they have other risk factors for osteoporosis. Early detection and

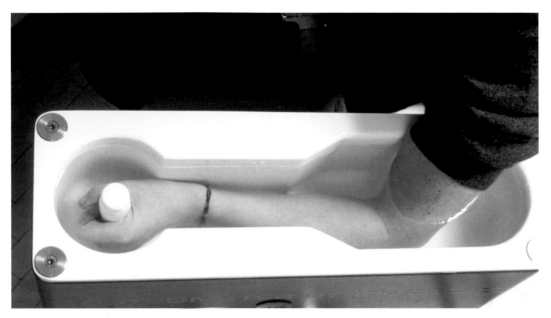

Bone scans can be used to check bone density in different parts of the body.

diagnosis is important for getting proper treatment and preventing further damage.

DEXA SCANS

Bone density is equal to the amount of calcium in the bone. The higher the density, the stronger the bone is. The most common type of bone mineral density test is called a dual-energy X-ray absorptiometry (DEXA) scan. This highly accurate test uses X rays with very low radiation to measure how dense bones are. It is safer than a normal X ray that is used to take a picture of your chest or check for fractures

Men are less likely than women to be tested for osteoporosis at regular doctor's visits. This makes it more difficult to detect the problem before significant bone loss occurs. Often severe back pain or a fracture already caused by osteoporosis is the reason men see a doctor and are finally diagnosed. Several treatment options are available for both men and women, but more research needs to be done regarding the differences between osteoporosis in men and women.

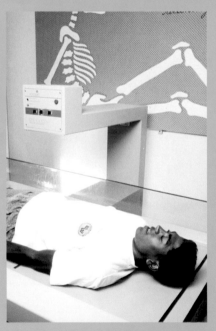

Men who are at risk of developing osteoporosis should also undergo bone scans. Early detection can help when treating diseases like osteoporosis.

because it uses about one-tenth of the radiation. It is also more accurate at diagnosing osteoporosis than normal X rays, which can only detect bone loss after 50 percent of the density is gone. Normal X rays may miss early signs of osteoporosis.

A DEXA scan usually measures the bone mineral density at the hip or spine. The patient lies on a table while the DEXA scan machine passes over him or her. It can also measure bone mineral density at the wrist or ankle using a special device that surrounds the arm or leg while the patient sits. It takes about thirty minutes to complete a DEXA scan. The X rays pass through the skeleton and the machine measures the

A doctor uses a special machine called an osteodensitometer to measure the bone density in parts of a woman's spine.

amount of radiation that was not stopped by the bone. Denser bone can stop more radiation than fragile bones. A computer attached to the machine calculates the density of the bone. Next, it compares the reading to what a healthy bone density should be. The result of a DEXA scan is called a T-score, and it represents the comparison of the patient's bone mineral density against the ideal peak bone mass for someone of the same ethnicity and gender.

Very negative T-scores mean poor bone mineral density. A T-score of at least -1 is considered normal. A patient with a T-score between -1 and -2.5 has low bone density. Osteoporosis is diagnosed for any T-score less than -2.5. Doctors often compare the results of several DEXA scans taken over time to see if a patient's bones are the same or if they are getting worse.

Physical Exams and History

There are other tests that a doctor will use along with the bone mineral density test to help diagnose osteoporosis. A physical exam and detailed medical history will give the physician information about risk factors such as family history, medications, intake of calcium and vitamin D, exercise, and previous fractures. Blood tests can measure levels of calcium, estrogen and other hormones, as well as other proteins that indicate the level of activity in bone formation. There are other bone tests that are different than measuring bone mineral density. During the test called a bone scan, a doctor injects a radioactive fluid into a patient. The body is then viewed using a computer and a sophisticated scanner to show differences in the radioactivity of various bone areas. It can detect new fractures and other problems, but should not be the only test used to diagnose osteoporosis.

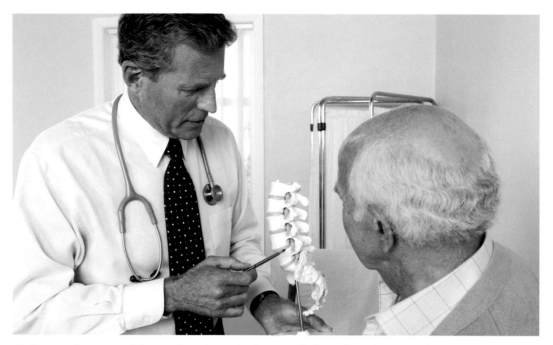

A doctor shows an older patient how the bones of the spine change as he gets older.

PREVENTION

Building strong and healthy bones is the key to preventing osteoporosis, and there are many things that you can do now to help prevent osteoporosis and fractures later in life. Make sure that you deposit enough calcium in your "bone bank." You can do this by eating a healthy well-rounded diet. Having a healthy diet means that you will be getting enough of your daily required vitamins and minerals—especially calcium and vitamin D. Stay physically active and focus on weight-bearing exercise to promote strong, healthy bones. Bones become stronger when you do activities such as running, soccer,

Other Bone Disorders

Sometimes people with fragile bones have a disease that is not osteoporosis. True osteoporosis is very rare in children. Fragile bones in children are usually caused by another condition or medication the child is taking. Children can usually recover and have normal bone mass if the condition is treated or the medication is changed.

Rickets and osteomalacia are both diseases caused by too little vitamin D and can lead to bone deformities and fractures. People with kidney disease are likely to have bone mineral problems that may appear to be osteoporosis, but should be treated differently. This type of bone disease is known as renal (having to do with the kidneys) osteodystrophy (bone disease).

There is a disorder called Paget's disease in which bones become weak and misshapen. In Paget's disease, the bone-building osteoblasts try to keep up with the bone-removing osteoclasts by adding bone as fast as they can. Unfortunately, the new bone they make is not normal—it is not strong or constructed in the tight, overlapping pattern that makes up healthy bone. Patients with Paget's disease end up with bones that are large but brittle or deformed.

Another bone disease that should not be confused with osteoporosis is called osteogenesis imperfecta, sometimes called brittle bone disease. This is a rare disorder that is usually diagnosed during early childhood. People with osteogenesis imperfecta have bones that break easily with very little force. This disease ranges from somewhat severe, with just a few fractures in a lifetime, to extremely severe, in which a person can suffer hundreds of fractures.

Drinking milk is good for your overall health and for keeping your bones strong.

dancing, and jumping rope. Do not smoke, because the chemicals in tobacco are poisonous to your bones. Studies have shown a direct relationship between tobacco use and decreased bone density. Smokers may also heal more slowly after breaking a bone and may have more complications. Even exposure to second-hand smoke may increase the risk of having low bone mass.

While getting plenty of calcium and vitamin D, exercising, and not smoking can help prevent osteoporosis, they are also important for people who have already been diagnosed with osteoporosis. It is important for people with osteoporosis to know that it is not too late to take action

Taking part in outdoor sports is a fun and healthy way to stay fit. You can get vitamin D from being out in the sun, and your bones get a workout from the physical activity.

and to protect their bones through changes in their diet and activities.

People with osteoporosis need to stay active to keep the bone strength they still have. They should not become inactive in the hopes of preventing a broken bone. A doctor or physical therapist can recommend safe activities to get the exercise the patient still needs. Generally, people with osteoporosis should avoid any high-impact activities that include bending forward from the waist, twisting the spine, or lifting heavy weights. Also, safe exercises that help improve balance, stability, flexibility, and strength will help preserve bone density and prevent falls.

People with osteoporosis should make every effort to reduce their risk of falling. Doctors recommend that people who are no longer steady walking on their own should use a cane or walker for stability. They should also wear shoes with rubber bottoms, and avoid high-heeled shoes. Rooms should be kept free of clutter to reduce the risk of tripping and falling. Safety bars can be put in rooms and bathrooms to help a person balance. Non-slip mats or rugs on smooth floors, on bathroom floors, or in the tub are also a good idea.

Physical therapy is often used to help people who have been injured.

TREATMENT

Preventing osteoporosis from happening or getting worse is important, but there are also several types of approved medications to treat osteoporosis. Bisphosphonates are one class of drugs that can help prevent and treat osteoporosis. They work by inhibiting (slowing or stopping) bone removal by osteoclasts. There are several different types of bisphosphonates that can be used in women and men. Bisphosphonates come in different forms, and can either be swallowed as pills or a liquid, or injected into the body.

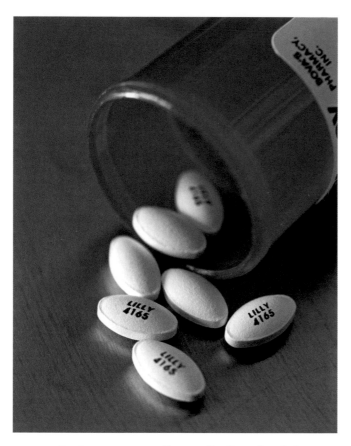

Doctors can prescribe medication that helps prevent or treat osteoporosis by reducing the amount of calcium lost from the bones.

Estrogen is another therapy that has been used to treat osteoporosis, but mostly in women. This hormone has effects on many different parts of the body. The problem with using estrogen as a treatment for one health issue is that it may affect other parts of the body, causing other health issues. Estrogen pills or skin patches have been used as a treatment for osteoporosis in women, but estrogen therapy has risks. These include increased chances of heart disease, stroke, and breast cancer. However, researchers developed a therapy that uses the effects of estrogen in a more specific, targeted way. This type of drug is called a selective estrogen receptor modulator (SERM) and it has different effects in different parts of the body. SERMs target the bones and are effective at preventing bone from being broken down. Female osteoporosis patients taking this type of therapy have been able to decrease the risk of spinal fractures. SERMs are swallowed in pill form and are less effective than estrogen at maintaining bone density. But SERMs seem to have fewer risks.

Bisphosphonates, estrogen, and SERMs all focus on preventing the breakdown of existing bone. Another approved drug for treating osteoporosis works by stimulating osteoblasts to make new bone and to repair the "potholes" in bones to improve their density. This drug is known as teriparatide, and is approved for use in both men and women who have a high risk of bone fractures. This drug is a modified form of the hormone produced by the parathyroid gland. The parathyroid hormone is involved in regulating calcium and phosphorus in the body and plays a role in maintaining bone health. It has been shown to stimulate new bone formation in the spine and hip. Teriparatide is taken as a daily injection that the patient can give himself or herself at home.

There are also ways to manage the pain associated with the disease, including pain medications and non-drug options. Physical therapy can improve mobility, and patients can also do exercises recommended by a therapist to improve their posture and balance. Yoga and tai chi are combinations of

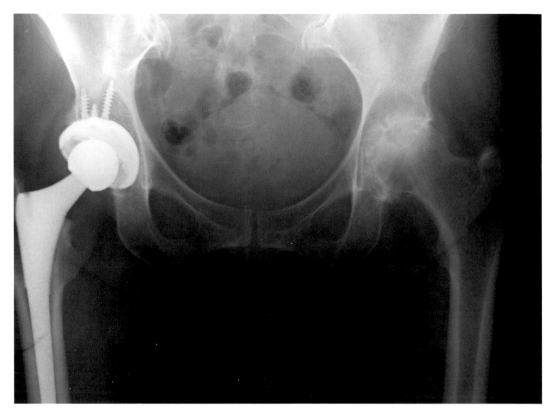

This X ray shows a patient who has had the bones in the hip replaced. The bones may have broken due to old age or osteoporosis. Surgery is one way to treat some bones affected by osteoporosis.

meditation, stretching, and holding certain body positions. When done correctly, these activities are not stressful on the body and can improve balance and flexibility. However, it is important for patients with osteoporosis to talk to their doctor before doing a lot of physical activity. Massage may also provide some relief from the pain of osteoporosis. Some people with osteoporosis have found that acupuncture works as well. Acupuncture treatment involves having a licensed acupuncture practitioner insert slender needles into the skin at different parts of the body.

It is likely that the treatment options for osteoporosis will increase greatly in the future. Many researchers are studying bone disease and trying to understand exactly what happens during bone remodeling. Discovering more about bone biology could lead to new drugs to prevent or treat osteoporosis. For now, it is important to remember that it is never too early or too late to improve your bone health.

It is never too late to establish good habits that can help you stay healthy.

GLOSSARY

bone marrow—The soft tissue inside bones, which contains many blood vessels and produces red and white blood cells and platelets.

calcium—An element that is found only in combination with other elements (compounds) and is essential for most plants and animals.

collagen—A protein that is produced in the form of strong, flexible fibers that is found in connective tissue and bones.

cortical bone—The dense, compact outside layer of bone that is mostly solid with only a few open spaces.

dense—Closely or tightly packed together. In bones, density is a measure of strength.

estrogen—A hormone that stimulates the growth of and maintains the female reproductive system, but is also a signal for promoting healthy, strong bones. Estrogen can be used to treat osteoporosis.

fracture—A broken bone or the act of breaking a bone.

hormone—A product of living cells that circulates in body fluids (like blood). They produce a specific effect on cells.

kyphosis—Extreme outward curving of the backbone that is due to multiple fractures, resulting in a rounded upper back.

menopause—The change in a woman's life when menstruation permanently stops. This usually occurs around age fifty.

nerve cells—Cells that carry electrical messages through the body and connect the nervous system with all other systems in the body. Nerve cells are also called neurons.

osteoblasts—Bone cells that are responsible for making new bone.

osteoclasts—Bone cells that are responsible for removing old bone material.

osteocytes—Bone cells that started out as osteoblasts that become part of new bone and take on the new job of sending signals to other bone cells.

osteoid—Newly formed bone.

peak bone mass—The strongest a person's bones will be in their entire lifetime. People usually reach this point between ages twenty and thirty.

physical therapy—The use of careful exercise, massage, or stretching done with the help of a trained professional to treat a disease or condition, or to help recover after a surgery or accident.

protein—Complex substances found in living cells necessary to carry out essential life functions.

remodeling—In bone health, it is the process by which old bone is destroyed and new bone is created.

spine—Also known as the backbone, the spine protects the nerves in the spinal cord and provides strength for the middle section of the body. The spine is made of bones called vertebrae.

trabecular bone—The inner layer of bone that is spongy and full of spaces that contain bone marrow cells.

vertebrae—The bones that make up the spine.

vitamin D—A vitamin that is needed for healthy, normal bones and teeth. It is found in foods such as fish-liver oils, egg yolks, and fortified milk. One form of vitamin D is a hormone that affects bone formation.

weight-bearing exercise—Any physical activity that makes your muscles and bones work against the force of gravity. During a weight-bearing exercise, the body is not supported by something, such as a bicycle when pedaling a bike or by water when a person swims.

X rays—Waves of energy that are blocked by dense materials. X rays can be used to create images of dense objects using special machines and film.

FIND OUT MORE

Organizations

National Institutes of Health
Osteoporosis and Related Bone Diseases National Resource Center
2 AMS Circle
Bethesda, MD 20892–3676
1-800–624–BONE or 1-800-624–2663
www.niams.nih.gov/bone

National Osteoporosis Foundation (NOF)
1232 22nd Street N.W.
Washington, D.C. 20037-1292
202-223-2226
www.nof.org

Books

Gold, Susan Dudley. *The Musculoskeletal System and the Skin.* Berkeley Heights, N.J.: Enslow Publishers, 2003.

Gray, Susan H. *The Skeletal System.* Chanhassen, MN: Child's World, 2004.

Hodgson, Stephen. *Mayo Clinic on Osteoporosis.* Rochester, MN: Mayo Clinic, 2003.

Sayler, Mary Harwell. *The Encyclopedia of the Muscle and Skeletal Systems and Disorders.* New York, NY: Facts On File, 2005.

Simon, Seymour. *Bones: Our Skeletal System.* New York: HarperCollins Publishers, 2000.

Web Sites

KidsHealth – The Big Story on Bones
www.kidshealth.org/kid/body/bones_noSW.html

National Bone Health Campaign
www.cdc.gov/powerfulbones

National Institutes of Health (NIH) Osteoporosis and Related
  Bone Diseases National Resource Center
www.osteo.org

Nutrition for Everyone: Bone Health
  Center for Disease Control and Prevention (CDC)
www.cdc.gov/nccdphp/dnpa/nutrition/nutrition_for_
  everyone/bonehealth/index.htm

Osteoporosis Tutorial
www.nlm.nih.gov/medlineplus/tutorials/osteoporosis/
  htm/_no_50_no_0.htm

INDEX

Page numbers for illustrations are in **boldface**

ABOUT THE AUTHOR

Gretchen Hoffmann enjoys learning and writing about many topics in health and science. She holds degrees in Biomedical Journalism and Biological Science and has conducted molecular biology and virology research at Cornell University in Ithaca, New York. Currently, she works as a senior medical writer at a medical communication company. In addition to *Osteoporosis,* Ms. Hoffmann is the author of two other Health Alert titles, *Mononucleosis* and *The Flu.* Ms. Hoffmann has also written articles for Scholastic's classroom magazine, *Science World.* She lives in New York with her husband, Bill, and their dog.